THE LABYRINTH
TAROT
LUIS ROYO

THE LABYRINTH: TAROT, by Luis Royo
ISBN 1-932413-24-3
© Luis Royo / represented by Norma Editorial
Published by Heavy Metal ®
100 North Village Avenue, Suite 12,
Rockville Centre NY 11570
Nothing may be reproduced in whole or
in part without the written permission
of the publisher
Printed in the EU

www.luisroyo.com

THE LABYRINTH
TAROT
LUIS ROYO

HEAVY METAL

INTRODUCTION

Tarot is a kind of wisdom stored in seventy-eight images or cards, divided into twenty-two cards in the Major Arcana, and fifty-six in the Minor Arcana. It is a labyrinthian language of combination, the origin of which has been lost in time.

Tarot is recognized as the pillar of Hermatism. Its symbols are an illuminating source that illuminates and drives the mind.

It is not a question of finding supporters or opponents, but to say that Tarot is a philosophical tool linked to astrology, cabala, alchemy, and magic which therefore means holds the key to first-rate occultist wisdom. In each image, as well as in the accompanying text, appear the astrological sign, its equivalent in the Hebrew alphabet and corresponding number. Their meanings derived from each of them must be sought in the different related sources, whose sheer extent makes them impossible to go through here. Similarly, the links to different mythologies are merely suggested and it is necessary to adapt the references to the actions and the meanings as archetypes.

Isaac Newton, the greatest scientist in history, kept hundreds of manuscripts and studies on lost civilizations. When John Maynard Keynes discovered these documents in Cambridge, he wrote, "Newton was not the first man of the Age of Reason...he was the last magician, the last Babylonian and Sumerian". Present day science has recently discovered the genetic code and shown that the synthetic DNA has a unique sequence according to its base structure in the form of a ladder. Depending on the arrangement of the genes on the chromosomes, the genetic map is created. As we can see this is the same path taken by the Tarot towards man in terms of his philosophical viewpoint. Some great names have been occultists, such as Eliphas Lévi, Papus (Dr. Gérard Encausse), P. Cristian, Fabre d'Olivet, Arthur Edward Waite and many more who have carried out serious studies on the symbolism and origins of Tarot, describing it as an instrument of knowledge.

While attempting to be as impartial as possible, and despite contradictions and confusion to be found in the thousands of books and documents dedicated to the subject, Tarot undoubtedly holds clues to the mysteries of mankind, and some even claim to the secrets of the Universe and human nature.

Like everything within it, the origins of the Tarot itself is labyrinthian and shrouded in mystery. Some research claims that it comes from the sacred scriptures of ancient Egypt. In the eighteenth century the Egyptian theory was supported by tracing it back to the god Thoth and the book of sacred teachings, patron of magicians and scribes. Studies carried out in the twentieth century, however, disclaim the Egyptian origin theory.

Some historians have discovered connections with doctrines such as Buddhism and therefore claim Indian origins. There are other texts supporting Arabic ancestry, coming from Arab merchants, or that during the eighteenth and nineteenth centuries Chinese round cards arriving from the East to Italian trading ports, such as Venice, were then turned into the Major Arcana.

Paul Foster Case claimed that Tarot was created in Fez, around 1200 B.C. when a group of intellectuals from different countries sought a universal language based on images in Morocco.

There are also theories that Tarot origin comes from gypsies. In the nineteenth century J.A.Vaillant, an expert in Roman culture, claimed the oriental influence in the cards came from the emigration of gypsies from India to Persia then to Europe.

Another version says it was invented by the Order of the Knights Templar, thus explaining the connection with the East and the symbolism in the Major Arcana.

In the eighteenth century, the cleric and mason Nicolás Court de Gebelin, was convinced of the Egyptian origin theory, going even further to claim that the Tarot is the "The Egyptian Book (Book of Thoth)" which still exists. In the nineteenth century, Alphonse Louis Constant, alias Eliphas Lévi, who defended the ancient Oriental origin theory, that it had been brought to Europe by gypsies and had Kabala links. Papus (Gérard Encausse) made the connection between the Major Arcana and the Hebrew numerical system. Contemporary writers such as Paul Huson have gone back to the gypsy and Egyptian origin theory, and Mouni Sadhu to that of Hermetic occultism.

This Labyrinth confirms that the Tarot holds such mysterious clues that it is capable of embracing different philosophical tendencies, without having to reject any of them as sources, since it brings together many common concerns.

Wisdom from all cardinal points is included in the images. Passionate defence of these different theories by Tarot scholars means that it has become an unprecedented source of wisdom. It is a major collection of symbolism represented in images, one of the most ambitious challenges to anyone working in the visual arts.

At the end of the Middle Ages, the Church was responsible for burning numerous decks of cards as they were considered to be pagan and sinful. The deck created by Visconti was saved from the flames, but is incomplete. Artists such as Alberto Durero have designed their own cards, throughout history their power of attraction has been evident.

The Marseilles Tarot, clearly based on Medieval sources and with no alterations to the original plates, is the standard Tarot deck.

Over four years ago I began a project to create a deck of Tarot cards. I have taken meticulous care to respect the wisdom contained within each image - the main reference being the 1736 Marseilles Tarot, which, as I have already mentioned, is the sharpest and most extensive version. The Rider deck, which appeared in 1910, Visconti's from the fifteenth century, Oswald Wirth's and many more (including some by contemporary artists) have of course all been present. However, my aim has been to create a Tarot for the present day, which continues to contain the most primitive hermetic codes and is not a personal interpretation. Although there are hundreds of artistic decks on the market, there are very few that respect the profound symbolism.

Unlike the garish Marseilles Tarot, the colour concept used for these cards is austere, in order to ensure they are easy to use so that communication between the cards and the reader is fluid as soon as they meet. The suits have also been modified - the coins have become pentagonal shields, because the gold coin which is represented by the Earth sign now has a more material sense, and not the ancient one of protection. The club, the sign of strength, which is in fact a branch, is substituted by a spiked club, as today nature has also lost its symbolism of strength and has become something which requires protection. From the goblet, the sign of water, waft vapours which suggest something mysterious in its interior. The sword, the sign of air, continues to maintain all of its symbolism.

The handling, reading and different ways of dealing the Tarot depend on the deck being used. In this book we will try to explore its rich esoteric symbolism.

On hindsight, if I had known the hours that would be spent, and the doubts that were to arise in the process of creating these cards I would never have taken on such a project, but now that it is completed, all I can say is that being submerged in this great universe has moved me to my core.

My hope is that it might also bring you something special, as it did for me. I leave you, then, with these pages of this ancient labyrinthian wisdom.

Luis Royo

300

THE FOOL

The unnumbered card of the Major Arcana.

It is the search for life's secrets. The eternal journey. The jester or fool who seeks experiences and desires perfection.

He also represents mystery and deceit. He is the breath which gives life and takes it away. The spirit. The path of impetuosity.

He is always behind all the other Arcana, and is the link in the circular chain, the cosmic movement of everything that exists. He is the darkest part of us which comes into the open under a different guise.

He is the mirror image, self-deceit, the path of delirium and frenzy.

His Hebrew letter is Shin, his symbolic number is 300 and his astrological combination is Air-Cancer.

He is a man carrying a bundle of clothes, who keeps on looking ahead, and takes no notice of the dog which bites him. His attitude signifies that he is not tied down by anyone, and that is why he is leaving. He is an adventurer. In the legends of King Arthur, Merlin appears not only as a wizard and a sage, but also as a cheat. As an archetype, the Fool expresses himself socially as the court jester.

The bundle, which the Fool carries on his back, contains his experiences: he does not abandon or forget them, but they simply do not control him. He walks with a stick over his shoulder, but the stick is really a wand symbolizing power. The Magician and the Chariot driver also carry wands, but they do so consciously with a deliberate firmness. The Fool, the dancer of the World, holds his wand so casually that one barely notices it.

Just as his number is 0, the Fool can really occupy any place and he jumps the gap between one line and the next.

The Fool represents surprise.

REALIZATION

He is number I of the Major Arcana.

He personifies will, creativity and symbolizes self-awareness. He brings with him astuteness, dexterity and originality.

He is the mantle of witchcraft, life and death, the image of all principles which emanate from absolute unity. The gateway to creativity, the Magician, with his symbolic tools, is the master who can use his skills to create beauty. His Hebrew letter is ALEPH, his symbolic number is I and his astrological combination is LEO-MERCURY. This Arcanum reveals to us that great individualisms really exist.

The mystics call him the Magician, but in vulgar language he is the juggler: essentially an active individual.

He is Hermes, the messenger of the gods, with the ancient Egyptian symbol of infinity linked to Hermes Trimegisto, the fusion of the divine and the personal; the serpent of eternal truth and knowledge; the skill of the written word.

He stands behind a table, on which there are several objects, each with their own symbolism. The wand he holds in his hand represents material transmutation and he is therefore able to achieve whatever he wants.

He is the wizard, the shaman who has cultivated his own willpower to the point where he is able to direct the fire that motivates him. At the same time, he remains open so that his Ego may dissolve under the violent attack of his spirit. We should not forget that the real magic lies in the images themselves, not in the explanations.

The Magician represents willpower - a will that is unified and directed towards objects. It signifies great strength, because all the energy is channelled in a specific direction. On his table lie the four suits of the deck and his simple belt symbolizes eternal truth, knowledge and duality.

Many scholars speak of the workbench or the square table, however the Italian artist Balbi, expert in esoteric philosophy, depicts the round table as symbolizing the Earth.

THE PRIESTESS

Represented by the letter BETH in the Hebrew alphabet.

Also known as "The door to the Sanctuary" by some occultists because it is the card of knowledge.

It is number II of the Major Arcana.

The Priestess is represented by Selene, the Moon Goddess. It is a water sign and astrologically linked to Cancer.

Her mantle, draped over the throne with the pointed ends is related to the horns of ISIS. This Egyptian goddess adopted the form of a bird of prey in order to conceive Horus and brought him up alone using shrewdness and magic.

She is the representative of occultist wisdom. Natural divine femininity associated with the arts and creativity. Also known as the High Priestess, she has her roots in the pagan Mother Goddess, a female deity dating to before Christianity.

The scroll of papyrus on her lap shows esoteric knowledge, associated with the Book of Thoth, or the sacred Jewish law. This parchment has also been connected to the book of the Apocalypse and with the Knights Templars' Liber Mundi and the Rosacruz. In the Marseilles Tarot she is shown with the papal mitre on her head. She is the Papess, which ties in with the legend of the female Pope Juana from the fourth century. In this version the mitre has been maintained but stylized to make space for a magician or witch's hat and bring us closer to her mystical talent.

Even though the Papess Juana and her death while giving birth during an Easter celebration is considered to be legend, her image can be seen in the Visconti-Sforza deck in the fifteenth century. Manfreda Visconti had already been chosen as the first female Pope a century earlier. The Church later finished with her by burning her at the stake. In fact this image can be seen in the Fournier Museum in Vitoria, Spain. In the Visconti deck available in the market this image has lost a lot of its beauty.

THE EMPRESS

Air. Ruled by the planet Venus, goddess of love and beauty. Astrologically linked to Gemini. Third card in the Major Arcana.

Femininity capable of transforming everything into harmony. It is the card of fertility, generosity and triumph.

It is interpreted as the representation of maternity, attraction, love and pleasure. Movement converted to evolution. Intelligence and creativity dominate, transforming and fertilizing her.

It is an air sign and in the Hebrew alphabet the letter is en GIMEL.

It represents mother earth. Material power is symbolized by her crown while her loose hair leads us to think of sensual love and fertility. The Eagle (the symbol used on sceptres and Roman standards, crusading knights, and royal and imperial emblems par excellence) appears on her shield as a sign of strength and power. The female figure holds the sceptre, also an imperial emblem, which has an orb of the earth and a cross at the end.

She turns nausea into desire. The strength of willpower. The one who looks at us from the throne of sexuality.

Here the female archetype shows us her accessible side. Unlike the archetype of the Priestess who represents the cerebral female aspect, the Empress talks to us of emotion. Life, according to the path of pleasure and feelings.

She is the representative of passion and sex. Even in the Waite-Smith deck she appears surrounded by nature to emphasize her sensuality and next to the river as the source of life.

In the Cabbala, number three also means the triangle, the man-woman-child association. In the Apocalypse according to St. John, there is a seated woman, cloaked by the sun. This sun is interpreted as being the fountain of life and creation.

Ⅱ

THE EMPEROR

The Emperor, ruled by Jupiter, with his white beard tells us of resistance and knowledge. It is card number III in the Major Arcana.

His crown also holds a military helmet, which links him to Mars, the God of War. He carries an imperial sceptre showing his power over the outside world and as in the case of the Empress, it is topped with an orb and a cross. Also, like in card number III, his shield is decorated with an eagle.

It takes the sign of the Earth and belongs to the letter DALET in the Hebrew alphabet. It is also related to Venus and Taurus.

Its world is physical existence, it symbolizes clear goals, dominion, authority, stability, mundane power and practical intelligence.

The physical and material masculine kingdom. The archetype is the image of the father. The unusual crossed legs position again points to the cross (the cross of the four elements and the four cardinal points) His semi-upright position suggests alertness, being ready for action. Mountains, indicating earthly power, can be seen through the window (like in the Arcana of the Empress).

In the Rider pack, the Emperor is dressed in armour and is sitting stiffly on his throne. This is interpreted as the rigidity of the rules of government and as sterility, as opposed to the abstract natural world of the Empress.

He is also associated with a trick played on Philip the Beautiful and his wish for the Pope to convert him into an emperor once he had finished with the Templars. Just before his execution, the great master of the Order of the Knights Templars, Jacques de Molay, called on Pope Clemente V, Guillermo de Nogaret and Philip the Beautiful to declare at the trial, where he accused them of being responsible for the disappearance of the Order. Within a year all three were dead, the curse having been fulfilled.

THE HIEROPHANT OR HIGH PRIEST

The Pope, also known as the Hierophant, the Priest presiding over the mysterious sacred people of Eleusis. Number HE, and his star sign is Aries. Astrologically related to Jupiter and Sagittarius.

This is a Fire card, it speaks of initiation into the occult but also of external doctrine. He is an old man with a white beard, crowned with the Papal Mitre as the High Pontiff and his mission is to bring Heaven and Earth closer together.

He is holding the triple cross of the papacy, the hierophant cross with a trunk, the channel through which the current flows to the underworld.

His glove also bears the Maltese cross, sign of a military and religious society as known as the 'Hospitallers', as they used to look after those wounded on the crusades.

Two figures are kneeling before him recognizing his wisdom and authority. In some decks these figures are one black and one white woman.

Seated between two pillars, between piety and severity, his right hand is raised in a sign of blessing. His two crossed keys are a sign of occultist knowledge, as well as being a sign of the papacy.

The High Priest transmits his esoteric knowledge; he dominates the external aspects of religion and the spiritual world, unlike the Priestess who deals with the inner world.

In the Visconti deck, he appears with a triple crown. In Aleister Crowley's deck (illustrated by Frieda Harris) he has a pentagram on his chest and he is on a bull, indicating balance and strength.

In some tarots, the High Priest figure has been substituted by Bacchus. In the Carlos VI deck the two figures are standing on each side of the Pope instead of in front of him.

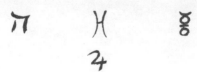

THE LOVERS

This Earth card takes us to the crossroads, the choice. Duality, purity and temptation.

It is number VI in the Major Arcana and is ruled by Taurus and is related to Mercury and Virgo in Astrology. It belongs to the letter VAV in Hebrew.

It represents the attraction of the senses, free will, the clutches of the principles of the masculine sex.

The outer skin gives way to inner doubts and leads us to the uncertainty dance.

In the centre of the image, a man is tempted by both sides and is abandoned at the dance to be put to the test.

This card is connected to the judgement of Paris, in which he has to choose between the three goddesses. The female figures in this case represent vice and virtue (in some decks the three goddesses next to Paris can even be seen, offering the apple of discord).

In the upper part can be seen Cupid preparing his bow to shoot his arrow through the eye so that love will enter the heart. Paris was blinded while considering his choice.

This card talks to us of the macrocosm and the microcosm and it shows us that what is on the inside and the outside is one and the same.

In other decks, like the Rider deck or the Minchiate Tarot from the seventeenth century, there is just a man and a woman being looked on by an angel, on a background suggesting the Garden of Eden. There are other interpretations, where one of the female figures is the mother and the proposed approach is to start on a new path or carry on under her protection.

In the tarot created by Jacquemin Gringonneur for Charles VI, two lovers join the dance then leave, while two angels are pointing at them with their bows and arrows.

THE CHARIOT

The Hebrew letter for this card in the Major Arcana is ZAIN. It corresponds to, number VII, and has clairvoyance and perception among its qualities. Its signs are Gemini and Water and the astrological link is with Venus and Libra.

The tarot itself, like the Book of the Apocalypse where the seven churches are mentioned, the seven seals, the seven trumpets, are all based on the number seven, which explains its importance in this Arcana.

This card is related to Ares or Mars, the son of Zeus or Jupiter and represents divine destruction as opposed to the stability of the Hierophant.

The four pillars of the Chariot represent the four elements: Earth, Air, Water and Fire.

The faces on the shoulder plates of the warrior driving the chariot takes to the past and to the future. It may also represent Phaethon on the chariot of the sun on his daily trip beyond Hell.

It is the archetype of the hero's victorious march carrying the triumphal sceptre. In some decks this card is called "The Triumph"

Shiva destroys the city of devils with the help of the gods. According to Hindu myth, they built a chariot with the heavens and earth, the Sun and the moon are used as wheels and the winds become horses. The lesson to be learned is we have to use everything in our power in order to obtain victory. In short, it is the vitality and capacity to take on new projects and challenges.

As always, the reference for this image comes from the Marseilles Tarot as it is the sharpest and most striking. It shows a front view of a chariot being pulled by two horses riding towards the viewer. In the Visconti deck, the horses have wings and they can be seen from the side. Lions and sphinxes can be seen pulling the chariot in other decks.

ℶ ♂ ♋

JUSTICE

Astrologically linked to Cancer, Mars and Scorpio. A water element and the corresponding Hebrew letter is JETH.

Number VIII in the Major Arcana means justice in all shape and forms.

The message is that all thoughts, feelings, all actions and strength used must be in balance with the Universe.

The goddess of impartiality, fairness holds the sword of rigour and precision.

She is the bearer of reward and punishment, severity and mathematics. She controls the monster of excess.

One of the Greek Titans, Themis, is Zeus's advisor and the personification of justice or the eternal law. She appears in the female form and was one of the four cardinal virtues according to Greek stoical philosophy. She is also associated with Athena or Minerva, the goddess of wisdom, the arts, science and industry.

Good and evil are weighed on her balance, looking for equilibrium. Her double-edged sword can condemn or save. The dishes of the scales represent the neutralizing binary element. If the balance is greater on one side the same weight has to be applied to the other to become level.

This card symbolizes equilibrium, rectitude, impartiality and harmony. It is an Arcana of power at the service of gods and men. It is the voice of conscience.

Some tarot decks show Solomon at the trial with his sword raised about to slice the child in two in order to find out the truth between the two women.

♏

ℯℯℯ

THE HERMIT

Number VIIII in the Major Arcana belongs to the fire sign and corresponds to Leo in the zodiac. It has an astrological link to Jupiter, Sagittarius and TETH is its Hebrew letter.

The number nine is the key to impenetrable knowledge, ascension, and spiritual transformation. It is the corner where the truth is sought; where nymphs of sensitivity and the fire of hermetic wisdom reside. The old man with the slow gait, vaguely illuminating the way, symbolizes experience and prudence. His light is the truth, the light of the spirit. His lamp is also known as the Hermes Trismegisto´s light, meaning hermetic wisdom. Astral capacity and physical knowledge, which once flourished in the Ancient Egyptian Initiation Temples. The might of the superior spirits is represented by the stick he is carrying. He trusts it to be able to continue his way along the path.

In antique tarots, symbols of the passing of time are present. His long beard tells us of wisdom and his rags, suggesting he is somewhere between a beggar and a friar, (in Carey's Tarot from the eighteenth century, the Hermit is called "The Pauper") communicate austerity in his actions.

Some call this Arcana "Hidden Light".

His path forms part of supreme Yoga, recognized as the two series of training to be carried out (which is too lengthy to go through here).

The theological texts of the Catholic and Orthodox churches basically coincide on the principles of both series.

We can also talk of inner light. Traditions in both the East and the West say that the perfect master prepares his last initiation for himself alone.

He represents Diogenes, who walks with the light of his lantern and a simple cloak. He is also related to Chronos (Saturn for the Romans), the Greek Titan of time. In the Orphic religious tradition, Chronos appears freed from his chains, reconciled with Zeus living on the island of the blessed. He is also connected to Bernardo de Claraval, author of the rules of the Order of the Templars. His number corresponds to the nine founders of the Order.

Major Arcana number X is the oldest known symbol - the Sphinx. YOD in Hebrew, Virgo and related to Mars and Scorpion astrologically. It is a water sign.

Also known as the "Windmill of the World" it is the card of transformations. The wheel turns raising everything than descending; one thing goes up, another goes down.

Osiris, God of Life, presides the top half of the Wheel. According to the Egyptians, the Lord of Fertility was the first to experiment the circle of life, death and resurrection. Karma in India, the law of cause and effect that rules our present and future lives.

Anubis, the jackal-headed god, climbs the wheel towards Osiris, testing the weight on the scale of the confessions of the dead.

Falling down the other side we see Seth, the god of chaos and disorder who ripped out Nut's uterus during his own birth, but he also serves as the counter weight, necessary in the order of Horus.

In Greek mythology it is connected to Ixion. Zeus felt pity for him after slaying his father-in-law, but nevertheless dared to fall in love with his wife, Hera. Zeus tied him to the eternally rolling wheel of fire in hell. The burning wheel of the condemned, which Satan spins eternally, is one of the most popular medieval concepts of Hell

On a human level, the three stages of the wheel represent childhood, maturity and decrepitude. In the prism of the Order of the Knights Templars, we would be talking about beginning, peak and downfall. This card is represented with Egyptian symbolism as it the Arcana with the clearest influence due to the image of the Sphinx.

They say that the Ancient Initiation Temple lies below it. This is where the 108 tarot cards, including 30 that remain undiscovered are said to adorn the walls. In the Fez Moroccan and Rider decks appear the four beings of Ezekiel the prophet: the angel, the eagle, the bull and the lion.

In the traditional tarots these elements only appear on the World card.

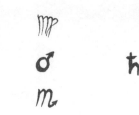

STRENGTH

Major Arcana number XI. Hebrew letter KAPH. Fire sign, astrologically Mars, related to Aries who dominates Leo.

On a human level it is the attraction of feminine strength. This Major Arcana card represents the supremacy of thought over brute force.

Its meaning refers to the conditions necessary for emergence and the application of evolutionary forces. The energy that overcomes all obstacles.

It also speaks of the purest state of sexuality.

It is also related to Cirene the nymph who lived in the wild in the forest protecting her father's flock from attacking beasts. Apollo fell in love with her after seeing her fight and tame a lion with her bare hands.

The sense of the strength of this Arcana also leads us to Samson's fight against the lion. His mother was barren but an angel promised her a child. In exchange he had to become a Nazarene, devoted to serve god and to never cut his hair. This is how Samson, hero of many great deeds, including the lion story, was born.

The Egyptian symbol of the eight on its side, representing infinity also appears here as well as in the Magician's card.

To highlight the sense of purity, the female form is naked here. Even though in the Marseilles deck the female image is clothed, she still evokes sweetness. In the Rider deck she wears a white tunic as a sign of purity. In the Visconti Tarot the figure is masculine and is about to strike a lion.

THE HANGED MAN

The Hebrew letter LAMED. Major Arcana number XII is a water sign and related to Libra and Pisces in the zodiac. Its numerical value is 30.

It is the sacrificial altar that lies between the past and the future. It is the balance between need and freedom. It is considered to be an initiation rite, an orphic mystery that uses sacrifice as a form of regeneration.

This Arcana deals with willingness for sacrifice.

The equilibrium that lies between liberty and necessity. Stagnation. Resignation.

The Hanged Man is suspended from a crossbeam supported by these two elements. There are six branches drawn on each side to represent renewed growth. He is tied and suspended by his left ankle as public punishment as applied in Renaissance times to humiliate knights who were thought to be too vain.

He is connected to Judas who was hanged after betraying Jesus. The Nordic god Odin was strung up from Yggdrasil - the ash tree of the world - after trying to find out mystical secrets. It is also related to Perseus on his sacrificial path.

Somewhat unreliable versions say that some alchemists and occultists believed that hanging upside down is a way of using gravity for liberating the energy from desire and transforming it, lowering it from the genitals to the brain.

The number XII ties in with the twelve tribes of Israel. This strange figure is tied by the ankle instead of by the neck. In Hebrew he is called ACAV, which is the etymological root of the name Jacob, father of twelve sons who founded the twelve tribes.

Quite a few decks, like for example the Rider Tarot, show the Hanged Man with a halo. However, there are no references to this in the older decks.

30

DEATH

This is Major Arcana number XIII, which is unmentionable. The Hebrew letter is MEM, air element, numerical value 40 and astrologically related to Saturn and Aquarius.

Eternity triumphs over the ephemeral. This represents the transforming principle, the eternal destructive movement that renews the spirit and is freed from the material. It even means physical death.

The sinister figure of Death walks through fields of putrefaction, pain, sadness and decomposition with his scythe. He leaves a trail of regeneration of new ghosts, men, gods, angels and devils.

What for some means the end, for others means the beginning. This is dealt with in great depth in the Cabala and Hermeticism. Popular literature considers this card to be negative but for the alchemists, putrefaction is one of the important processes in the overall scheme of things.

After the fall of Jerusalem, Ezekiel had a vision where the bones of Israel arose and were covered again by flesh.

Its number, XIII clearly links it to the beginning of the Order of the Knights Templar, with the council of the city of Troy and the involvement of Saint Bernard, Ezekielad of Claraval. The number thirteen is also linked to the disappearance of the Templars. The most frequently repeated element of this card in tarot decks is the scythe. The skeleton uses it to harvest, preparing the field for renovation. The corpses left in its wake are of young and old, rulers and subjects. Even after reaping, new shoots of grass spring from nature, symbolizing regeneration. Life is born from death.

It is also associated with the Moirae or Fates, who regulate the lifespan of each human being from birth to death with the help of the thread spun by the first, gathered by the second then cut by the third when existence comes to an end.

In almost all tarots this card is visually overwhelming, with the skeleton on its feet as in the Marseilles deck, or on horseback as in the Jacquemin Gringonneur version for Charles VI.

TEMPERANCE

Earth element, star sign Scorpio and related to Saturn and Capricorn. Major Arcana number XIV. The Hebrew letter is NUN and numerical value 50.

A winged female figure pours liquid from one glass to another: this liquid symbolizes purification, strengthening and inspiration. This card is related to Dionsios and Bacchus mixing the wine with water.

This card speaks of creative genius. The ability of combining spontaneity and knowledge and of connecting different aspects of life. The word temperance is derived from the Latin 'temp-are', which means 'to mix' or 'adequately combine'.

It is the Arcana of harmony and conciliation between the mental and spiritual plane with the worldly, material plane.

It is fusion. The ponds of spirituality are at her feet and the mountains and trees of worldliness are behind her.

Hebe, the Goddess of youth, who was in charge of serving nectar to the immortals, dances with the Muses and the Hours to the sound of Apollo's harp. Temperance is also connected to Iris, who symbolizes the arch named after her in Spanish (Arco Iris is Spanish for rainbow), and with the union between Heaven and Earth, between gods and man.

She came down to Earth using her wings in order to give divine messages to mortals.

This Arcana is also connected to Ganymedes, the Trojan prince who Zeus in the form of an eagle, kidnapped to make him a cupbearer to the gods.

His task was to fill all empty cups with the nectar of immortality. The female figure has a rose in her hair, which is the symbol of secrets - the Mystic Rose of the Templars. The rose was brought to Europe from Damascus.

In the Crowley deck, Thoth is called "Art". In the most famous tarot from the eighteenth century, the Etteilla deck, there is an elephant behind the female figure.

50

THE DEVIL

Its Hebrew letter is SAMEJ. This Major Arcana is number XV, numerically it is 60, Sagittarius and astrologically related to Venus and Libra.

The Devil figure, with two horned goblins, one male, one female at his feet, dominates this card. They represent the forces of Nature in a bipolar positive negative aspect; the idea of good and evil in man's mind. They are pictured chained up to symbolize the capture of vital energy.

This card has the double meaning of powerful passion and exuberant excesses. With this, success on earth is negotiated.

It is the card of temptation and vice. It takes us to success from a material and carnal point of view, even to extremes.

The big goat is in the middle. Vital energy emanates from him. The image of Baphomet is linked to the Templars and some associate it with the wisdom that also comes from the Hebrew Kabala. According to the controversial Eliphas Levi, it represents the sign of initiation, the hieroglyphic figure of the great Divine Tetragram.

Worship by the Templars of the god Braphomet (considered to be pagan) was one of the gravest accusations against them. It is also related to the spirit of the Divine Light, Mitra.

In many tarot decks the Devil card is clearly an image of Braphomet. However, in the Marseilles deck, it also the medieval Christian concept of Satan, and let us not forget that Satan is in fact a member of the celestial court, his name in Hebrew "Hasatan" means adversary or accuser.

The Devil in the Marseilles deck wears a sort of round breastplate, which is related to the serpents who curl round the hero. His dark wings are sensorial flight. His horns signify creative energy. His claws show us his desire to trap the earthly world. He defends and controls the Universe with his sword.

In the ancient Piedmont Tarot, the sword is substituted for a spike with two points.

THE TOWER

Number XVI of the Major Arcana. AIN is the Hebrew letter. Capricorn is the zodiac sign and it is astrologically related to Mars and Taurus. Earth card. Numerical value 70.

It is also the demise of Adam and Eve and their expulsion from Paradise-on-Earth. The Tower of Babel. The destruction of the Temple of Jerusalem, and it also somehow incorporates the decline of mankind.

The symbolism of the decay of human construction has made it a frequent cause for concern.

The Tower, or Castle shows man's power of conquest and worldly settlement. The image of chaos reflects mankind's fear of not being able to find and measure our capacity. The Tower of Babel tells us about this and its image has been represented throughout different historical periods in paintings.

This card is related to the fall of the Order of the Knights Templar. A thunderbolt destroys the Tower and small spheres fill the sky. They say that the spiritual material falls to earth, the Hebrew Gods. The biblical God is always surrounded by light and lightning. The Greeks also considered it a symbol of regenerating potential.

The part of the Tower that is falling looks like a crown and shows the viewer the fall of splendour. Two falling human figures signify the collapse of existence.

The Tower itself can represent an immobile impenetrable being which, under the influence of external forces, loses the crown. Their thoughts in human form, fly off looking for new values.

It signifies radical change and destruction. In the Thoth deck, the celestial eye watches over descent of the falling figures to the flames of Hell.

70   𐤏   ♏

♂

THE STAR

Major Arcana number XVII, numerical value of 80. Air sign, which belongs to Mercury and is related to Gemini. The Hebrew letter is PEH.

The great Star dominates this card. It is the lucky star, the morning star, evening star, Venus and Aphrodite. The wise man's guiding star.

This figure is related to the Babylonian whore in the apocalypse of St. John.

(Babylonians worshipped the stars). But above all it is the Egyptian Goddess Isis, with her cloak of stars. The lady of magic, the wise tongue whose word never fails. Using witchcraft, Isis brought Osiris back to life long enough to be able to conceive her son Horus.

It is also linked to Mary of Magdalen and with Mary, the mother of God. The Templars referred to it as "Mary, the Star of the Seas". Masons consider the Star to be the main manifestation of light, the centre of mystery.

When drawing with a compass and set square, it represents regenerated man in all his radiance.

Its brilliant circle directs the spirit and inspires.

Its light guides us. It shows hope and it will bring a message from our unconscious on which path to follow.

In this card we have the naked female figure, adorned only with purity and sensuality. The Water of Life pours from her two jugs, in two directions, material and mental. She has one foot on the ground and the other is submerged in the water. A small bird of sensitivity and love is watching her from a tree. In this Arcana we can see both celestial elements, stars in the skies as well as nature represented by trees, the earth and water. In the delicate Milanese Tarot from the nineteenth century, the clouds come down from the horizon to reveal the star filled sky. In the Minchiate deck there are various figures, kings and commoners below the great star.

THE MOON

Number XVIII in the Major Arcana is one of the most controversial. The Moon, TZADEK is its Hebrew letter. Its sign is water and is related to Aquarius and Cancer. Numerically it is 90.

The elements contained in the image make it one of the most enigmatic Arcanas.

The moon is in its first quarter. There are two guard dogs below. They say that these two dogs represent Philip the Beautiful and the Pope Clement V. In the background there are earthly fortresses. The lunar power over water, rivers and seas is reflected by the image of water at their feet. It ends with an image of a crab, astrological symbol associated with the moon.

Card number XVIII is related to the Goddess Artemis or Diana, personification of the moon and the goddess of hunting, and guardian of springs, currents and wild animals.

It is also connected to Hecate, goddess linked to darkness, who controls crossroads.

She wanders in the shadows followed by a pack of howling dogs. The invention of spellbinding and the protection of witches and magicians are also attributed to her.

The night card. From the world of fantasy, which also leads to darkness, to the world of deceit and lunatic illusions.

The moon does not emit light, it merely reflects the light from the sun, the ghostly illumination fills the world with deformed shadows. Some tarots call it "the Sunset". The moon's symbolism is very complex. Feminine principle by nature and therefore related to fertility. It speaks to us of biological rites with its continual growth and waning, like the birth and death of each day.

In the form of a segment or full like a woman. God and the Moon is an indivisible unit and it is the physical appearance of the feminine divinity in the world of man. Temples honouring different gods from ancient civilizations held the Moon as a primary symbol and the priestesses were in charge of celebrating magical fertility rituals taking the lunar cycle into account.

Shiva, in his role as transformer, had a half moon as an emblem. In the Hindu faith, it is the way of the ancients.

Some older tarots, like the Visconti deck, have a female figure accompanied by the moon on this card.

THE SUN

It is fire. The Hebrew letter is KUF, the sign Pisces. Related to Leo and linked to Aries in astrology. The numerical significance is 100.

The Major Arcana of the Sun, of energy and light.

Ra the sun god in Egyptian mythology, creator and ruler of the Universe. The daily journey of the Sun, the cycle of eternal renovation that represents the victory of life over death. During this journey god fought against the forces of chaos. The Sun God is also known as "the Big Cat" and the Egyptians evoked his presence by calling out " Male cat who killed the serpent of chaos"

It is also related to Horus, the God of the Rising Sun, of the sky, light and goodness. One proclamation to Horus is "Lord of action; he with the strong arm".

Apollo, enemy of darkness, Greek God of Day and the Sun who delighted the gods playing his lyre.

It is the divine fire stroking the world. The Great Circle of Light. Happiness, talent, sexuality, genius.

It is considered a positive and constructive card. Clarity, vitality and energy.

In the image we can see the powerful Sun at the top inundating everything with energy and generosity, spreading its purifying fire. At the bottom a wall makes reference to its powers of protection.

Two human figures enjoy the caress of the sunlight; they are entwined enjoying the heat.

In the Visconti deck, in this Arcana, only one figure appears on a cloud, with a sun in its hands, which looks more like a mask. The Rider shows us a solitary child on horseback in front of a wall full of sunflowers.

200 ○ ♄

JUDGEMENT

The Major Arcana number XX is planet Saturn, Earth sign and astrologically related to Virgo.

The Hebrew letter is RESH and its numerical value 200.

The day has come. Nothing can hide behind the celestial powers. The angel of the Apocalypse plays its trumpet. It is associated with St. Michael who keeps planets in their orbits.

The Angel of Judaism, Christianity and Islam. The Archangel led his faithful troops and defeated Lucifer.

His call invites man to rise towards a more meaningful existence and to self-reflection. The tree figures in the lower part of the image are reborn due to the effect of celestial energy, and they are elevated to a higher plane.

It is the path to reintegration, regeneration and astral transformation.

Pluto, God of the Dead is among Saturn's children. In the ancient as well as contemporary tarot decks, the figures below are placed in coffins in order to emphasize both this idea and that of the final judgement.

The trumpet calls to our inner and outer selves. Re-birth.

It speaks of the departure from Earth to celestial worlds; of the final moment when we will be judged for our deeds. Death and resurrection, preached by different civilizations and religions. The Angel comes from the heavens surrounded by a circle which symbolizes the beginning and the end, birth and death. The Absolute, The Alfa and Omega, eternity beyond all time and space.

Michelangelo created the most striking image that could be represented in this tarot card. His great Final Judgement in the Sistine Chapel.

ħ   ∿   ☉

THE WORLD

This Arcana wears the crown or emblematic ribbon of the whole tarot.

This is the last of the Major Arcana Cards. Under the sign of the sun, the synthesis and the centre of all the stars in the planetary system.

Fire. Astrological influences from Saturn and Leo. Some also connect it to Jupiter.

Card number XXI of the Major Arcana. The Hebrew letter is TAV. The glorious body is represented by a shamelessly naked female figure. The mandorla around her, the almond of glory, the end of the Great Scheme. The magic crown called "the World" This card gives way to the Minor Arcana via the Pentacles. It speaks of absolute truths that have no need of protection. Supreme manifestation of mental perception.

The essence of the metaphysical bases of the Earth is the ARCANA ITSELF. The exterior self united with life forces.

The victorious ballerina in the middle of the card moves her vaporous veils of gestation with both hands, dominating the binary mystery, she seems joyful, allowing us to glimpse her material and sexual reality. Her dance is also the occultist initiation in the India of Shiva, the king of all dancers, the triumphant dance of the god of the Yogis. The manifestation of the supreme.

This figure is in the opposite position to the Hanged Man, indicating its inverse relationship to the number twelve.

There are the four mystical animals surrounding her - the four "living beings" of the prophet Ezekiel. The Hermetic school shows them as Air, Water, Earth and Fire. The different powers in the Kingdom of Nature. The four Cardinal Points.

Perhaps the old tarot deck which most distances itself from the symbolism of this card in the Marseilles deck, is that of Visconti, where there are two cherubs holding a globe containing a castle.

400   4   ⊐   ⊙

I

PENTACLES

Astrological link Earth - Capricorn.

Adam was created from mud, thus showing the importance of the physical world. The coin or pentacle tells us of the measure of man, and of material protection. It also indicates the magic in earthly creation.

In this tarot, the pentacle (the five-pointed star of Hermes, God of Alchemy) is also a protective shield. In the ancient Visconti deck, the ace of coins, is shown with a shield.

The suit of pentacles, usually represents power, protection and wealth, not only on a material level but also of intellect and technique. The pentacles or coins are the diamonds of the international decks of cards. The Ace is the triumph in golden words. It is the gift of the Earth: the magic is in life itself and we are inundated by nature. The wisdom of the path chosen in order to be seated at the great table. The miracle of unity, a life full of joy. Orgasm. Delight, ecstasy, flesh, wealth.

In the delicate Royal Fez Moroccan Tarot, like Rider's and other contemporary tarots, the coins are pentacles.

II

PENTACLES

Earth sign, astrologically related to Capricorn.

Worry, lies. Nothing is what it seems. Behind the laughter everything is fake and grey. Both shields teeter on their sides, placing balance in danger. Although in other decks, the card numbers are represented together with the figures, in this tarot I have remained faithful to the minimalist Marseilles design, for its clarity at the moment when the cards are laid out.

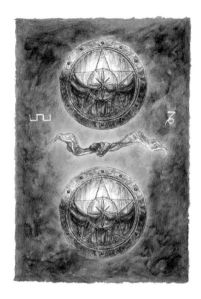

III

PENTACLES

Earth - Capricorn.

This card is skill and know-how; the perfect roundness of the coin. With this card we enter the world of effort and construction. In the Rider deck, a monk and an architect with plans of the church appear.

IIII

PENTACLES

The Earth and Capricorn are its signs.

Misery and dark greyness fill the soul, even though the harmony of the composition calms the spirit. The four coins float around the well-known mountains but are unable to roll down.

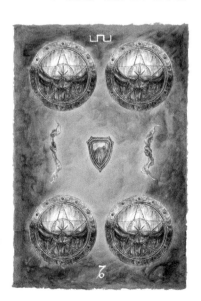

V

PENTACLES

Astrological link: Earth, Taurus.
Energy abounds within us without a means of escape. Poverty of the spirit. Earthly world is unsteady. There are clouds on the horizon.

VI

PENTACLES

Earth sign, astrologically linked to Taurus.
The honey from the theatre lights, the curtain opens to reveal generosity. It communicates sharing without disregarding the position of the individual.

VII

PENTACLES

Astrological relationship Earth, Taurus.
The symbol of having obtained something forbidden using great effort. The coming of the hour of glory and success.
With patience and continuous effort the dream of the VII of Pentacles will come true.

VIII

PENTACLES

Earth sign related to Taurus.

Everything is on its natural course. The world before us is on a horizontal plane. Everything is alive, although sometimes on a real plane and at other times in fantasy. Creative ability based on tradition. The five pentacles refer to skill and the initiative to create and learn.

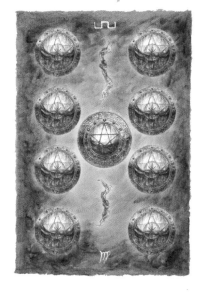

VIIII

PENTACLES

Earth - Virgo.

The well-worn path. Peaceful sleep. Eyes that can look gently into our interior. The nine of pentacles has faith in its destiny, Triumph on earth is deserved. Numbers XVIII, XIX, and X would be linked to the higher octaves. In astrology, the planets Uranus, Neptune and Pluto would have the same role of expansion and accentuation in a deck of forty cards as they do in the astrology of the planets.

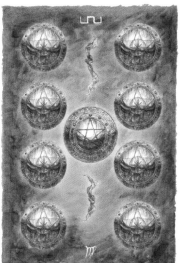

X

PENTACLES

Astrological link: Earth, Virgo.

Capacity for enjoyment. The X of Pentacles harvests the rich fruit from both the interior and the exterior. The limits are set and there is sufficient space. Tribal attitude, where you know your place.

JACK OF PENTACLES

Earth sign related to Capricorn.

The young, bright messenger girl. With her head held high she will confront the new day with determination and a desire to learn. Her gaze takes on the past and new ideas.

Her hair blowing in the wind will bring us the scent of a sweet missive. She gets ready to face the world with confidence. In the Balbi deck she skillfully plays with a ribbon between the coins.

Her breasts are bared to the wind, but sometimes her dreams get lost in the sheer immensity of the sky and her extravagant figure will roam around the field of scattered illusions.

In the daily battle of life a new "self" is found everyday and the old self dies.

KNIGHT OF PENTACLES

Earth sign, related to Capricorn. Aquarius and Pisces in astrology. Tenacity. Bearer of the way to follow the path.

It dominates and simplifies the exterior, knowing how to choose which side of the mountain to gallop down , and so relax his horse. His shield and protective pentacle accompany him with profound earthly wisdom and the paths lead him towards the strength of a practical world. His perseverance and opportune walk takes him through even the darkest forests without the need for rest.

Obstacles die in his hands; his young, bright energy illuminates and flattens out the rocks.

This is one of the cards in the Visconti deck that has not been found.

QUEEN OF PENTACLES

Earth and Capricorn.

Expert in the magic of nature and the power of life, her body weight leans on her shield and material pentacle.

The Golden Queen takes communion with the world, offering us the sensuality of her expression. She is about to be seated on the throne to receive honey from caresses. She knows and believes in herself, after her coronation she will let her mantle fall to the floor to confidently display her thighs.

She exercises an energetic and generous control of the rooms of her palace, she talks to us of creative interest.

Opulence and luxury. Limitless sexuality in all its forms. Earthly corpses cannot deal with such a generous interior which reaches the point of lust. Thoughts cannot travel up to the clouds; they remain trapped under the skin.

KING OF PENTACLES

Astrological relationship, Earth and Capricorn.

His white hair does not remove from the energy in his gaze (in the Marseilles Tarot, we can recognize this energy).

His is the strength of a triumphant king, but at the same time he is reclining, accustomed to his success. He has no need of a crown, he is generous and knows he is king. His success has justified his life so he now relaxes enjoying his reign. Even though his pose suggests attentiveness and energy, he is patient, reserved, loyal and faithful to his dominions. He is seated with his feet firmly on the ground and feels pleasure from the earth. Experience: He shakes the storms from his back. Flames of prosperity based on character and intelligence. At the same time, he is the king most shrouded in darkness.

I

CUPS

Under the sign of water and related to Cancer, Scorpio and Pisces.
Water, ruling sign for this suit, is what brings the seed to life so that it will sprout up from the ground.

The Cups are linked to the Church and to the Holy Grail. King Arthur's knights remained united due to the presence of the Holy Grail but the kingdom disintegrated once it disappeared.

They represent love, imagination, joy and peace. The cups are about dreams, enjoyable emotions, love and passion. They are also about instinct, emotional development and the unconscious.

In the international decks they are the hearts. The I of Cups, or the sacred goblet, brings harmony between man and his world, it contains the elixir of life. The upper crowned part tells us of subliming feelings and senses. It has also been linked to a tower or fortress of the Order of the Knights Templar. In various decks the construction is represented. The solid base powerfully supports this treasure of mankind. The tarot readers who use the 40 card pack call it "The House". Legend links the Grail to the emerald that fell off Lucifer's forehead when he fell from the heavens. This also ties up with the eastern Third Eye tradition and its meaning of eternity.

Whether in the form of the fountain as in the Visconti deck or the Holy Grail (with the presence of the dove of the Holy Spirit) as in the Rider deck, the I of Cups gives us the gift of joy.

II

CUPS

Water sign astrologically related to Cancer.

This card speaks of the ability to be in harmony with others, with affinity. It is the triumph of the heart and how to relate to others. The sweet taste of the grape.

It shows two identical cups symbolizing mutual respect.

The Rider deck has a winged lion and Hermes Caduceus over the two lovers. The wings of the spirit and the lion of sexuality.

III

CUPS

Water - Cancer.

The success of the flesh, extreme pleasures, the conscience of worms and walking a path. The Goddess of Fortune brings us happiness. Spring comes and the clouds disappear.

Love of the world and sharing the wonders of life. Although Waite, from his moralistic viewpoint, spoke of this as being the card of excess and physical enjoyment, it is the card of happiness and pleasure.

IIII

CUPS

Astrological link: water and Cancer.

Also known as "divine dissatisfaction".

The road is full of stones and sodden clothes. Dreams have died in the brain and the box has to be reopened.

Our entrails suffer from misunderstanding of others and the world is full of frustrations.

V

CUPS

Water sign related to Scorpio.

It is the map of the crossroads. The fire has gone out, the retina has forgotten beauty and a new light has to be kindled. The fingers no longer feel and have to search for new sensations. The dark storm sweeps away and poisons idealistic feelings. The feet will touch the ground again after facing broken hopes.

VI

CUPS

Water and Scorpio.

The bag full of memories is opened.

Nostalgia and yearnings come spilling out. The idea is to retrace one's footsteps and to sleep under the trees.

The melancholy of a memory. A glance backward without turning into a statue of salt. The lonely soul struggles to find a new direction.

VII

CUPS

Its signs are water and Scorpio.

The emblematic number seven will make dreams come true. With the clear goal of desire, you will be able to sit down at the table with your loved ones. Creativity and the mind are in their youth, high above the stars, where sweat is made of sweet tears. The unexpected makes us smile. All doors to happiness will be wide-open and we will be filled with emotion.

VIII

CUPS

Astrologically water and Pisces
We will find a new life on the planet of the giants, which used to scare us in the past. Lost out in the sea of words, where only thoughts lie in the depths, we seek spirituality.
With a broken heart we set out on a journey towards the unknown, leaving the present behind.

VIIII

CUPS

Water - Pisces.
A balanced image drives us towards hope. The path widens and the rocks turn into sand. There is a blue sky and joys hang freely from the trees. The joy and the celebration of our earthly being. The desire for pleasure. Inner security and joie de vivre. Relaxation and satisfaction.

X

CUPS

Astrologically connected to Water and Pisces.
The qualities of this suit reach plenitude with the ten, the highest number in the Minor Arcana. It therefore shows us emotional security. Sensuality and spiritual enjoyment.
Sitting at the door with dreams and desires happily dancing around.
The sun shines on soft mountain and peace entwines itself around our fingers.

JACK OF CUPS

Water sign astrologically related to Cancer.

An offering to others. Sensuality approaching affability. Shy and distant while being seductive and sensual. In the ancient Florentine Minchiate Tarot, the Jack of Clubs is represented as a maiden.

Moving seductively but the eyes half closed, she offers her vessel filled with anarchic vapours - a mixture of passion and apathy, infidelity, sensuality, shyness and aggressiveness.

With a soft, friendly gesture she speak sweet words while her uncovered belly will provoke fire (in the Balbi deck, a butterfly on the cup speaks of this gentleness). The interior and the exterior are constantly covering each other up.

THE KNIGHT OF CUPS

Astrologically related to Cancer, Leo and Virgo, it is a water sign. The romantic and seductive dark knight lights up the path to passion and sex with his torch. He fills the space with thread and weaves a spider's web ready for his conquest.

He appears relaxed from the darkness and whispers in our ear. The snake's forked tongue that bewitches us.

Calmly he lowers his head to follow and study the tracks left on the soft path to find traces of his desire. His powerful steed is ready for you to mount and ride off with him over the horizon.

♍ ♋ ♌

QUEEN OF CUPS

Water sign related to Cancer.

Over the throne, she is sensitivity and sensuality between the vapours of art.

The Companion Queen. She turns scratches into soft strokes. An expression of poetry.

While one hand strokes the cup of senses and feelings, the other holds the sword to protect them. Her universe wraps us in gentleness while responsibility is lodged between her breasts. Although she appears to be relaxed, she is always tense and ready to defend her throne and castle.

Waite talks of the cup created by the Queen herself, which is an indication of the success of the imagination.

KING OF CUPS

This card is related to water and Cancer in astrology.
He holds the vapours himself and lights up the throne room.
A powerful king who spreads himself out.
The wind of generosity and good sense. The hundred faces of effort. With discipline and imagination he has achieved his goal.
Completely absorbing, he displays his cauldron of intoxicating light, contemplating his self-made universe.
The heat from his cup and heart determine the laws.

I

SWORDS

Air sign related to Libra, Aquarius and Sagittarius astrologically. "Ruwach" in Hebrew means "spirit" or "wind". With the air element, swords take us to the essence or soul of the matter, but also clearly to death. The suit symbolizes struggle, war, conflict and misfortune. These cards represent spiritual combat.

Spades are the swords of the international deck.

The ace of Swords with its sparks flying off the edge of the blade shows energy and power and solidness in taking on any projects. Determination. Discovery of the centre. Snakes are crushed by the steel.

The final victory. The discovery of the "self".

The single sword is usually depicted with the crown to add to its symbolism, like in the Marseilles, Florentine Minchiate and Rider decks.

II

SWORDS

Air - Libra.

The balance of mental power. Duplicity. The gaze set on two paths.

The two rival swords tell us of two different worlds, making us hesitate as to which hilt to grasp.

Air particles reach us from distant lands.

III

SWORDS

Air sign related to Libra.

The written folios require your stamp.

Playing in the shadows, it threatens the tyranny of reason over the senses. The attraction of chaos. Behind the light.

Pain. In the Rider deck the three swords pierce the heart.

IIII

SWORDS

Astrological link: Air - Libra.

The four sabres tell us of immobility, the feverish sweat of illness, isolation and loneliness.

Exhaustion. Closed eyes. The truce of the prairie and the desert. Between the corners.

V

SWORDS

Air sign related to Aquarius astrologically.
The bars of your thoughts.
The eternal inner journey. Regret.
The five swords symbolize dark menacing clouds hovering over us.

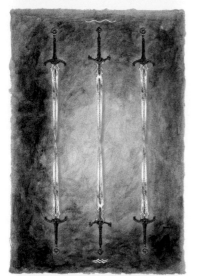

VI

SWORDS

Astrological relationship: Air - Aquarius.
It is time to get going; brute force.
Change. Searching for new horizons.
Rotten fruit falls from the trees. Tears, unpleasantness in every corner,
the air has become sickly and wrath walks the fields.

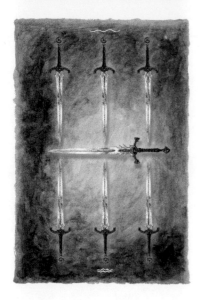

VII

SWORDS

Air - Aquarius.
Hope. External perspectives sharpens even though the path is hard.
Knavery and astuteness heal the wounds and the battles come to an
end. Droplets of water on the brow are not of sweat but from the cool
mountain spring.

VIII

SWORDS

Air sign related to Gemini.

A closed place where no light or oxygen may enter. A place where you find and recognize nobody, not even yourself.

The steel bars of the sabres surround us and fill us with desperation.

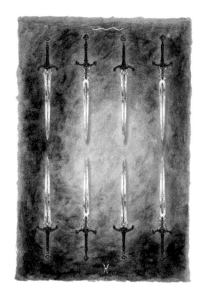

VIIII

SWORDS

Air and Gemini.

Tears. The shame of nakedness. Empty thoughts. Big storms are approaching, and suffering and pain deepen.

Exhaustion and impotence threaten us with the blades of the nine swords.

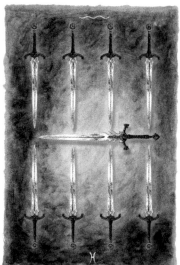

X

SWORDS

Astrological relationship: Air - Gemini.

The union of ten swords can only bring pain, grief and misfortune, sorrow and even lead us to death.

This card means the end.

Empty fruitless fields. Walking produces wounds and the horizon darkens.

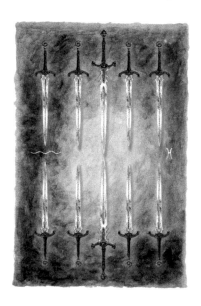

JACK OF SWORDS

Air sign astrologically related to Libra.

Observant, alert and independent. The new mountains of life are scrutinized almost like a little girl who wants to play with the new world she has just discovered.

Her frivolity attract us to her soft hips. Even in the Marseilles Tarot deck, the pageboy represented in the card has a seductive well-shaped waist.

She observes with malicious eyes; she tells us how she will take over our dreams. Her rival gaze, beyond the stars and time itself.

Her sexuality awakens, adapting itself to space.

KNIGHT OF SWORDS

Astrologically related to Libra, Scorpio and Sagittarius.
Air sign.

Arrogant and brave, the knight faces the winds with his sword
in the air to vanquish the storm. His youth means he has not
yet known defeat and he challenges his enemies passionately,
to the point of cruelty. His furious steed is willing to take him
to even the most difficult rocky peaks. Daring. Thoughts that
know no danger. To arrive at the very edge of the precipice.
Sights set directly on the goal.

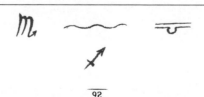

QUEEN OF SWORDS

Air sign astrologically linked to Libra.

The so-called card of "the Widow" is the Sad Queen. The King died and her knight lover was lost in the forest lured by the fairy song.

As she sits on her throne she meditates on how the painful experiences have made her wise. With her sword of intellect she scrapes the steps of confusion, fear and doubt.

Even though she holds her head down she remains on the throne. Spiritual and self sufficient, she tries to kill the demons of fate. A hundred ropes of jealousy surround her body.

THE KING OF THE SWORDS

Air - Libra.

His acute eye is fixed on his dominions and he boldly sends us his strong mental energy and wisdom. His vertical sword is an arrogant demonstration of his strong convictions and intelligence with arrogance. He leads his soldiers into battle himself. Somewhat younger than other kings, he doesn't even have a beard in the Marseilles Tarot. He shows that he feels active and ready for action. Although in the Visconti deck none of the kings are bearded, he is the only one wearing armour and is ready to fight. Even the Balbi deck has him in a standing position. The castle walls are strongly built and the protection is solid but the territory is rough and you have to be prepared to defend it. Useless words and dreams are kept on the shelf.

I

WANDS

Fire sign associated with Aries, Leo and Sagittarius.

The suit of Wands or clubs refers to the power of nature, its renovation and growth, but it is also linked to fire as a catalyst, the divine spark of creative imagination and work.

It is the equivalent of clubs in the international decks. The Ace of Wands or "the Staff" is the symbol of authority, vital force necessary to pass through the gateway to a new path (the design containing points supports the significance the symbolism of power and energy).

There are references to power, justice, force, success and fertility. With its help we grow and develop our inner self.

Each step of the ladder of life can be climbed up in safety with the wand.

It is the time to move on with enthusiasm.

It is the place where new fruits grow and dreams become tangible. The radiance from one of the wands shines on the new inner order.

II

WANDS

Astrological link: Fire - Aries.

Clouds shed raindrops with messages.

This card refers to a moment of pause, of indecisiveness.

There are also interpretations of the II of Wands, which make reference to maturity and the consequences of aims, to the careful and neutral possibilities and even to charisma.

III

WANDS

Fire - Aries.

Practical knowledge, harmony, union, the embrace.

The statue that opens her eyes with determination. The search for continuous thought.

With great effort, the path and goal in life is sought with her. Stable relationships, sense of protection and good outward intentions.

IIII

WANDS

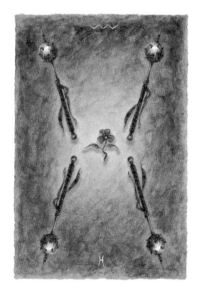

Fire sign related to Aries.

The IIII of Wands tells us of feeling welcome and of welcoming others, peace, harmony and happiness.

It also indicates inactivity, patient waiting, staleness and even boredom.

Thoughts are occupied by escape from the labyrinth. Energy is withheld.

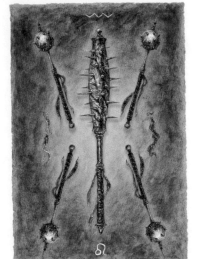

V

WANDS

Astrologically related to Fire and Leo.

The five wands presents themselves as great obstacles and bring controversy. Emotional adversity.

A stone-filled sack on our backs. The head below the feet. The skin full of scratches.

Provocation; strength is measured out either in frivolous disputes or in the need to fight for new convictions.

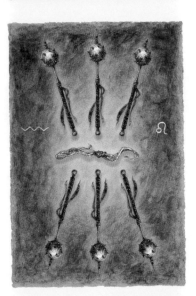

VI

WANDS

Fire and Leo.

This card speaks to us of advance, of slight improvement and carrying slowly on along the path. Although light and pleasant, this is a card of triumph. Desires will be fulfilled. Alternating between laziness and hard work, also the result of effort. Desire to emanate optimism and confidence in oneself. Fields full of wheat. The wind whistling in your ears that dries your tears.

In the traditional 40-card fortune-tellers deck this is known as the "Love Card".

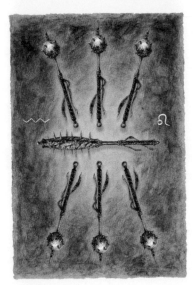

VII

WANDS

Fire sign astrologically related to Leo.

The triumph of the mind. Obstacles successfully overcome with intelligence.

The VII of Wands is read as meaning a conciliatory attitude. Constructive and open-minded ideas.

The inner devils have succumbed to the bottomless well; summer heat brings a glow to the cheeks and brings good news.

VIII

WANDS

Fire - Sagittarius.

Events change course. The VIII of Wands shows us that something is about to happen.

Hope. You can see love arrows and good vibrations in the sky.

Thought waves are smooth and constant. On awakening we will see another horizon. We are ready to tread the path, while barely stepping on it.

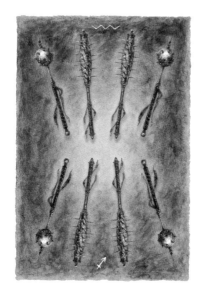

VIIII

WANDS

Astrological link: Fire and Sagittarius.

This is the moment of emptiness in the preparation of a new project in order to carry it out with greater effort.

The VIIII of Wands threatens us with conflicts and setbacks.

Firmness, obstinate conduct, stubbornness.

The darkness does not allow us to get a glimpse of the smiles. The devils show their teeth and we stop the machine.

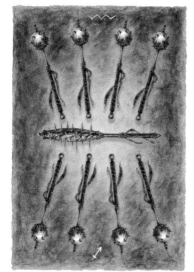

X

WANDS

Fire sign related to Sagittarius.

This card speaks of the effort needed to achieve a goal, and of the need to solve problems swiftly.

The X of Wands squashes us. Commitments and problems.

Overdemanding, overwhelming , a lack of perspective, oppression.

Dreams are heavy and cannot fly. Too much pressure impedes movement.

Search for power impregnates the body with selfishness.

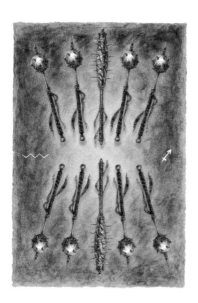

JACK OF WANDS

Fire sign astrologically related to Aries.

Still at rest, without having chosen her direction but with her sights set on starting out.

Her light dress is laid out with the embroidery of creativity and the potential of savoir-faire.

Her goal is clarity and objectivity. Even though she has not started walking, she analyses the direction her life is going in. Both the maiden in the Marseilles deck and the page in the Rider tarot are gazing towards the horizon with a relaxed demeanour.

KNIGHT OF WANDS

Fire sign related to Aries, Taurus and Sagittarius.

The soul united with the birds. The door opens onto an unknown world. Thoughts as clear as rays of light, filtering through a wood.

His home and castle are behind the forest.

The knight saddles his steed to set out on his journey. His fire sign leads him clearly towards movement and he waves his stick roughly to show his enthusiasm for adventure.

QUEEN OF WANDS

Fire - Aries.

Her protective glance embraces us.

Confident and relaxed, she allows us to wander around the palace where all desires are fulfilled; home to where the goblins who fill the sacks with dreams; where an orgy is revealed behind a curtain. This is the Queen who places the wand between her sensual legs with pride and dignity. In both the Visconti and the Rider decks, the Queen of Wands is the one who sits with her legs apart.

⋀⋀⋀

KING OF WANDS

Astrological relationship: Fire - Aries.

The Honest King. He studies us from his throne. The strength of his will has placed him in this privileged position. Upright, expert in controlling his dominions with his willpower.

A creative and powerful king, knowledgeable of the truth. He holds the wand or club with confidence and faith in his inner self. His takes his place on the throne with energy and that is where everyone will find him, exercising his authority.

The sinister side of this card means it can also symbolize the maturity that creates slaves and lusts after adolescents.

BIBLIOGRAPHY

Illustrated Books

WOMEN

MALEFIC

SECRETS

III MILLENNIUM

DREAMS

EVOLUTION

PROHIBITED BOOK I

PROHIBITED BOOK II

PROHIBITED BOOK III

PROHIBITED SKETCHBOOK

CONCEPTIONS I

CONCEPTIONS II

VISIONS

Trading Cards Collections

FROM FANTASY TO REALITY

FORBIDDEN UNIVERSE

THE BEST OF ROYO

SECRETS

MILLENNIUM

PROHIBITED

Portfolios

WARM WINDS

III MILLENNIUM

TATTOOS

CHAINS

PROHIBITED SEX

Others

THE BLACK TAROT

STRIPTEASE POSTCARDS

POSTERS

WOMEN BY ROYO

PLAYING CARDS

ACKNOWLEDGEMENTS

It is not necessary here to give an exhaustive and weighty list of the dozens of volumes consulted for this work, both by well-known authors, some of whose names appear in the introduction, and other more contemporary writers. But I would like to extend my thanks generally to all those who have drawn or written about the Tarot, because together they have achieved an unprecedented symbolic and hermetic richness.

I would also like to thank Pilar San Martín and "Anica" Martínez for their advice on the practical handling of the deck and to the memory of old Mari, the gifted fortune-teller, inseparable from her cards, for the hundreds of occasions on which she gave me the pleasure of her wisdom.